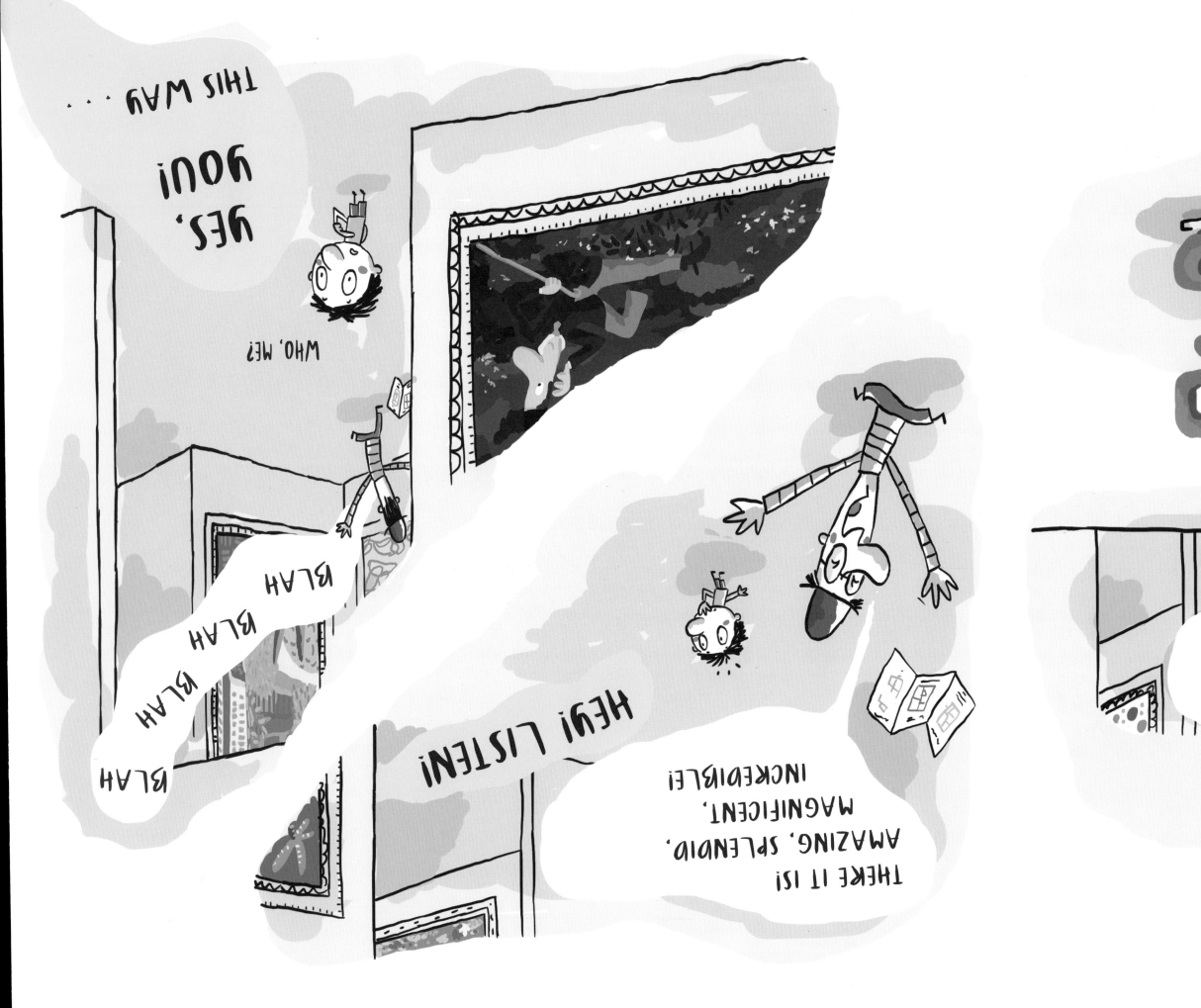

MUSEUMS are places where important and interesting works of art are kept and displayed so that they can be preserved. They are open to the public so that everyone can view and enjoy these extraordinary works.

Our museum is **a huge maze** full of stairs, galleries, and hallways. There are many rooms where artwork is arranged by artist or style. **It's easy to get lost!**

Today we are going to visit a museum—
a museum of modern art.

And what is MODERN ART?

In the past, artists used to try to represent the things they saw with the utmost accuracy, depicting them as they were in real life. You could almost say they were taking photographs with brushes and chisels, instead of cameras.

But about 150 years ago, a group of artists began to paint and sculpt in a different way, because they didn't want to copy reality. **Art changed. Modern art was born!**

Visiting a museum of modern art is a lot of fun. You can find sculptures hanging from the ceiling, figures that move and make noise, or works of art that have been painted using handprints or by splattering paint with a brush.

In our museum, you will find works inspired by the **great masters of modern art**. Now we will introduce you to some of them. Get ready to follow the mazes . . .

~IMPRESSIONISM~

Impressionist painters wanted to show
the effects of light as it shone on nature
by depicting the **impressions** they noticed.
They painted landscapes using **pure colors**
and rarely used black for shadows. They
loved working outdoors with their canvases
and palettes.

Claude MONET

preferred to paint the same landscape
at different times of the day to capture
the changing effects of the light.

Edgar DEGAS

did not go out into the fields or roam
the streets, as his friends did. He liked to
paint ballerinas rehearsing.

There were also **female impressionist painters.**

Mary CASSATT

painted mostly portraits of women
with their children in scenes of
everyday life.

. . . and there were many, many more!

FIND YOUR WAY THROUGH THE WATER LILIES . . . TRY NOT TO FALL IN THE WATER!

~POST-IMPRESSIONISM~

Like the impressionist painters before them, the post-impressionists painted **intense, lively** scenes using **bright colors**. The artists each had their **own style** that distinguished them from the others.

Paul CÉZANNE

represented things with simplified forms, using cubes, cylinders, and other geometric forms.

Georges SEURAT

painted thousands of dots that together give shape and color to things. His paintings are easy to recognize because they are full of little dots. This style of painting was called **pointillism**.

Vincent van GOGH

painted landscapes, portraits, and flowers using a very personal style that was based on short, thick brushstrokes and bright colors.

Paul GAUGUIN

went to live on the Pacific island of Tahiti and painted portraits of women sitting in fields or on the beach. They wore traditional costumes and had flowers in their hair. His colors were also bright and vivid.

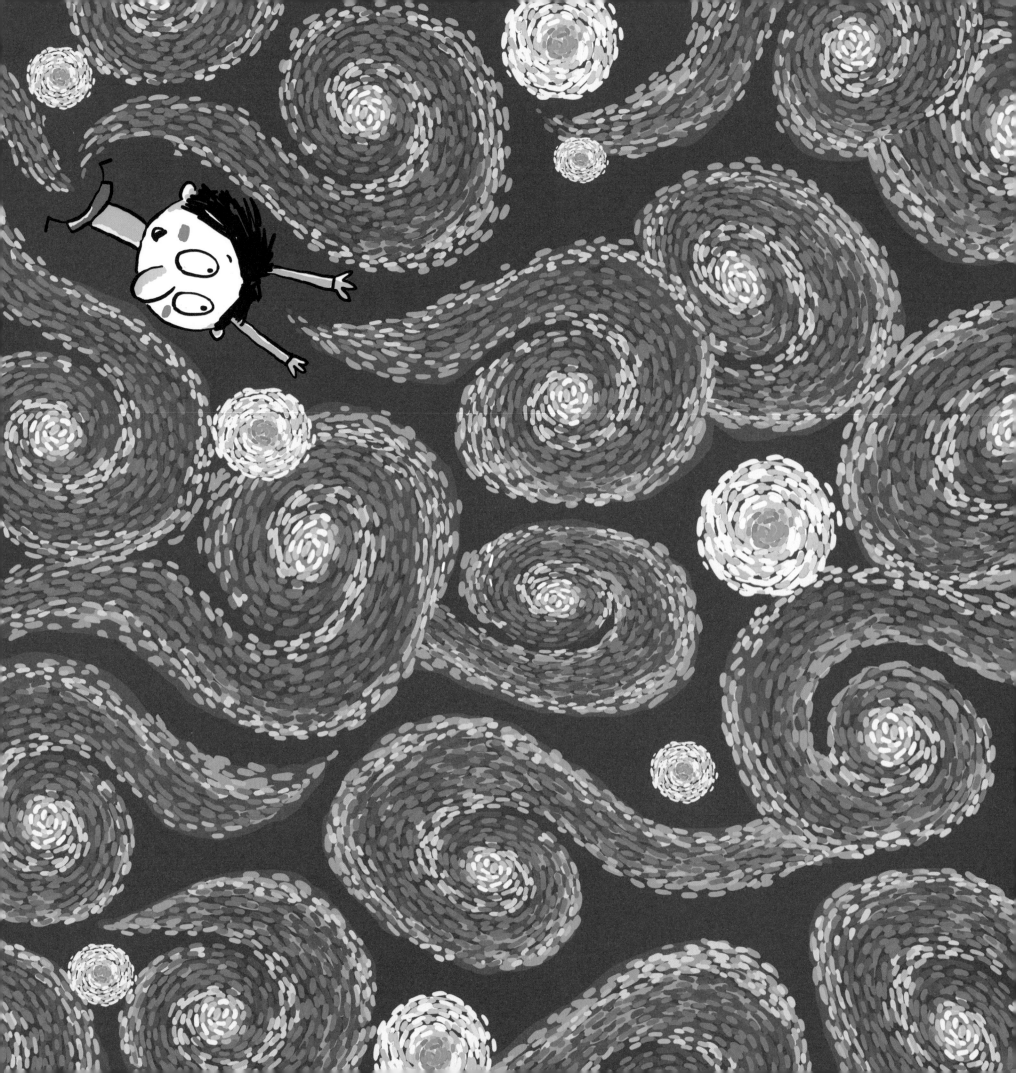

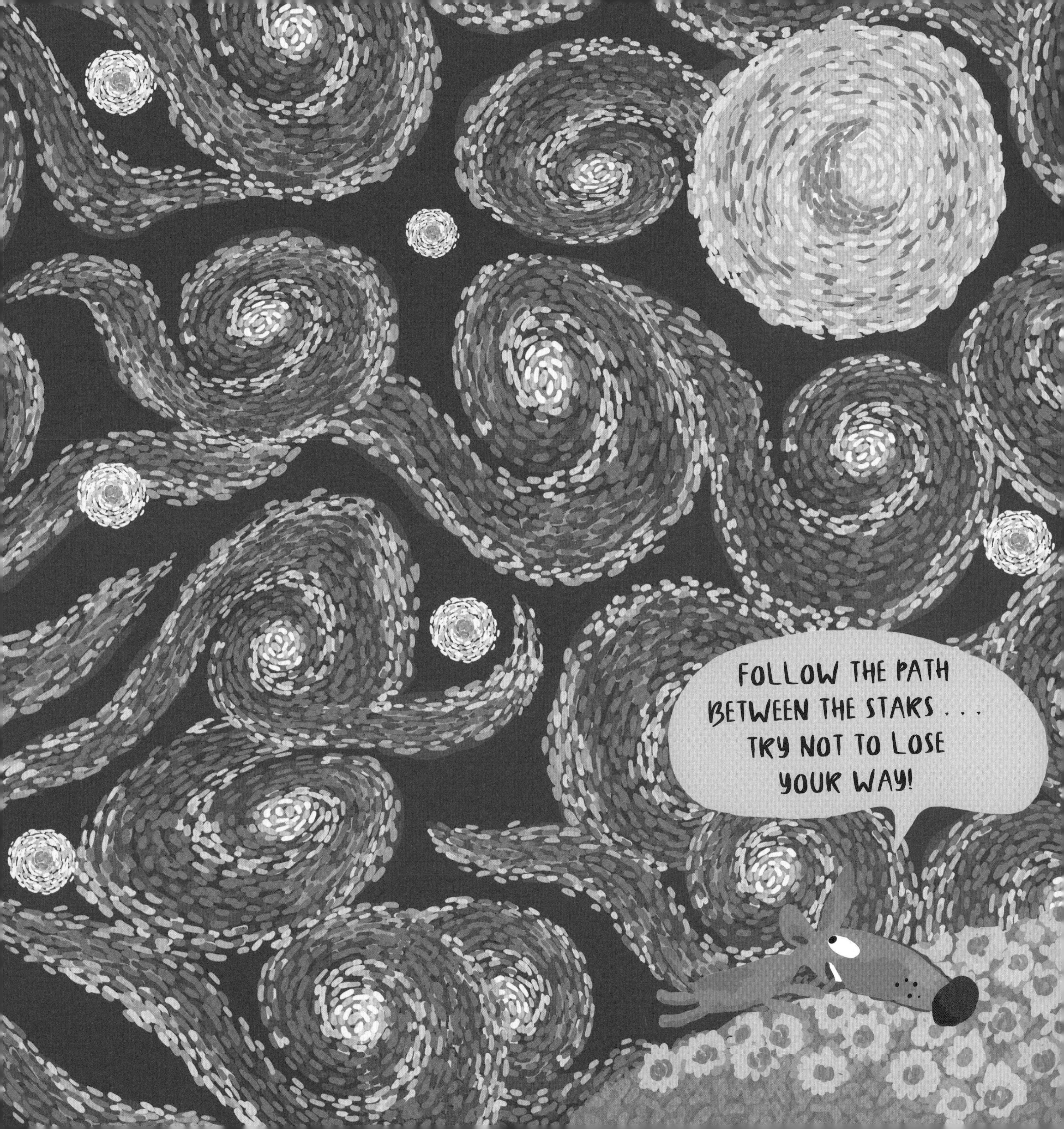
FOLLOW THE PATH BETWEEN THE STARS . . . TRY NOT TO LOSE YOUR WAY!

~EXPRESSIONISM~

Expressionist artists wanted to express **their feelings** in paintings or sculptures. They used **darker colors** and more **aggressive forms**, almost as if they were angry. Their paintings are sometimes very sad.

Edvard MUNCH

painted *The Scream*, a very famous painting of a person desperately screaming for a reason we don't know.

Paula MODERSOHN-BECKER

was a pioneer of expressionism. Although she died young, she left behind a very original collection of works.

~FAUVISM~

Fauvism is an expression that comes from the French word *fauve*, which means "beast." These artists were "beasts" who painted in a **free and wild way**, using spots in **bright colors**.

Henri MATISSE

painted many pictures of dancers, women, landscapes, and rooms with large windows. At the end of his life, he created some very interesting pieces by cutting and gluing pieces of colored paper.

André DERAIN

traveled to the south of France to paint landscapes. He represented the light of these places using very intense colors.

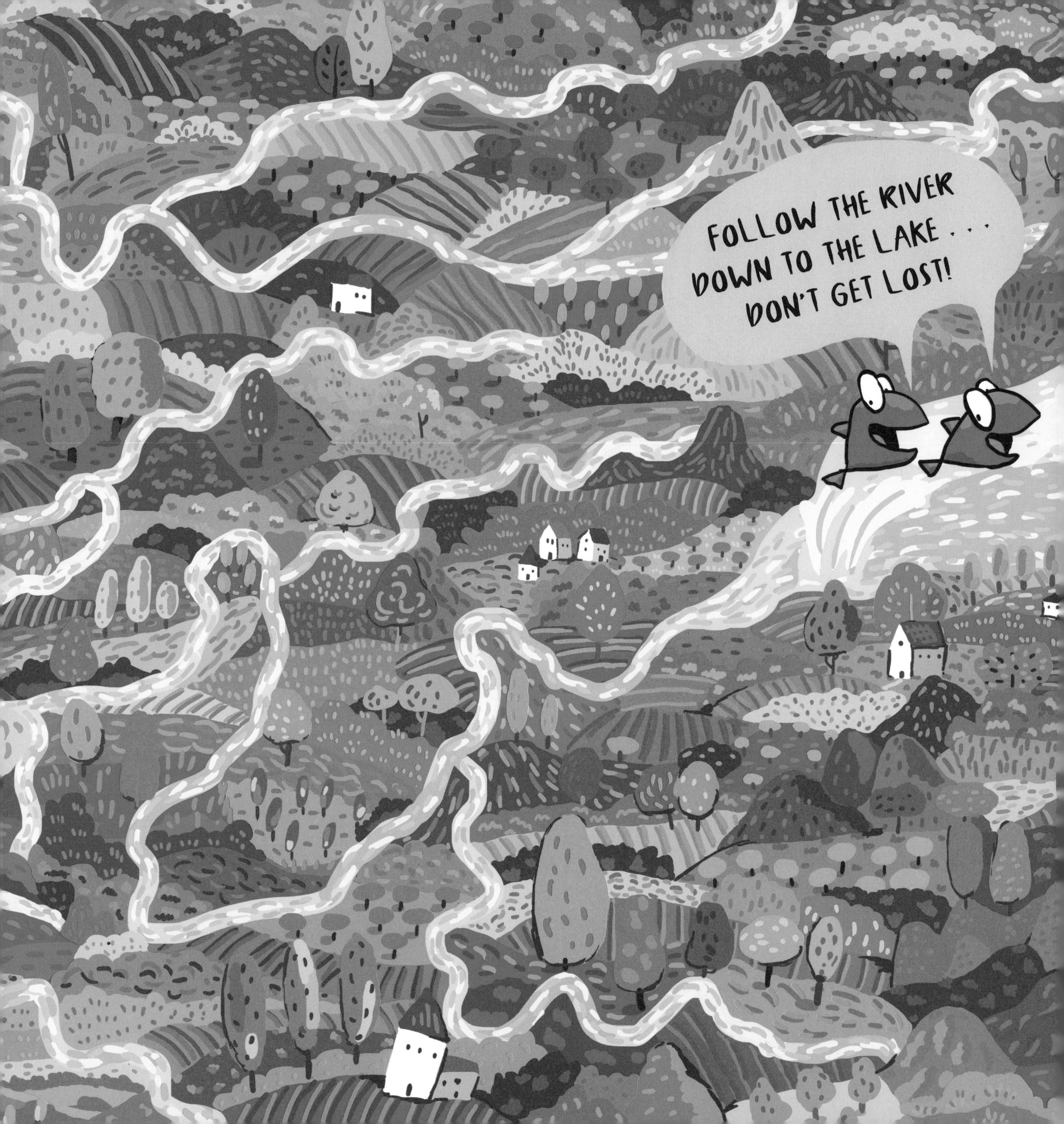
FOLLOW THE RIVER
DOWN TO THE LAKE . . .
DON'T GET LOST!

TA DAAAA!!!

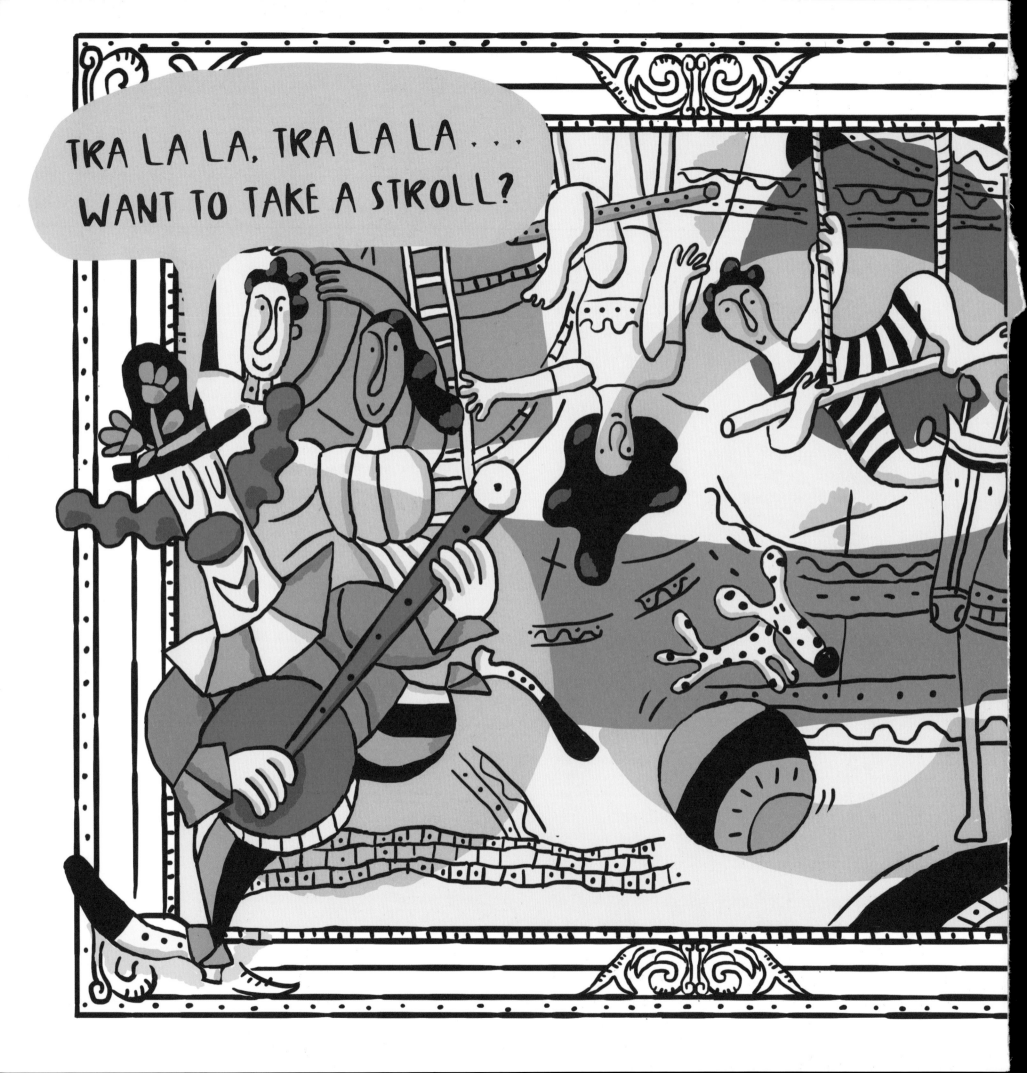

~CUBISM~

Cubists painted reality by depicting objects and people from **different perspectives at the same time**.

Pablo PICASSO

began to paint cubist pictures when he had already worked in other styles. He was always looking for new ways to make art. He was one of the first artists to use the collage technique.

Georges BRAQUE

was the other great experimenter of cubism. Elegance and balance in composition were always important to him, and these attributes characterize all of his art.

Liubov POPOVA

was a Russian artist who was as daring as Picasso. She painted still lifes and landscapes and designed dresses, ceramics, and theater sets in a her personal cubist style.

Constantin BRÂNÇUSI

was a sculptor and photographer. In his sculptures, he applied the cubist technique of representing things from various perspectives.

AWESOME!

~ SURREALISM ~

Surrealist painters thought that you had to let your **imagination run wild**: that's why they tried to **paint dreams**. In their works, they depict **images you could never see** while awake.

Joan MIRÓ

painted birds, eyes, women, and skies with stars and planets. He used only a few colors, especially yellow, red, blue, and black.

Paul KLEE

filled his paintings with fantastical creatures and intricate cityscapes using geometric figures and harmonious ranges of colors.

Leonora CARRINGTON

was a painter and a sculptor. She liked to paint fantastical or magical scenes, some taken from fairy tales.

René MAGRITTE

painted surprising situations featuring people and objects represented with great realism. In his paintings we can see, for instance, a large apple floating in the air or a man that has a hat but no face.

OOOOOOH!

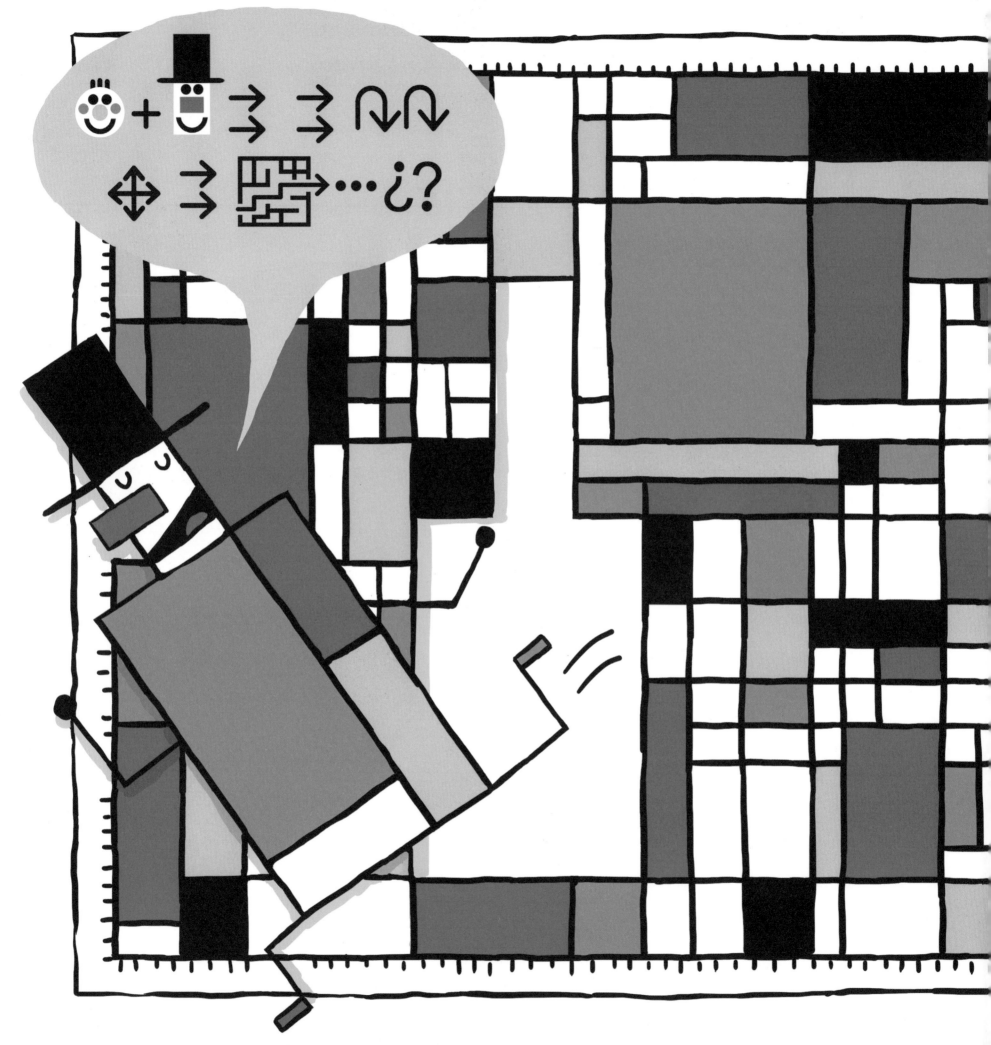

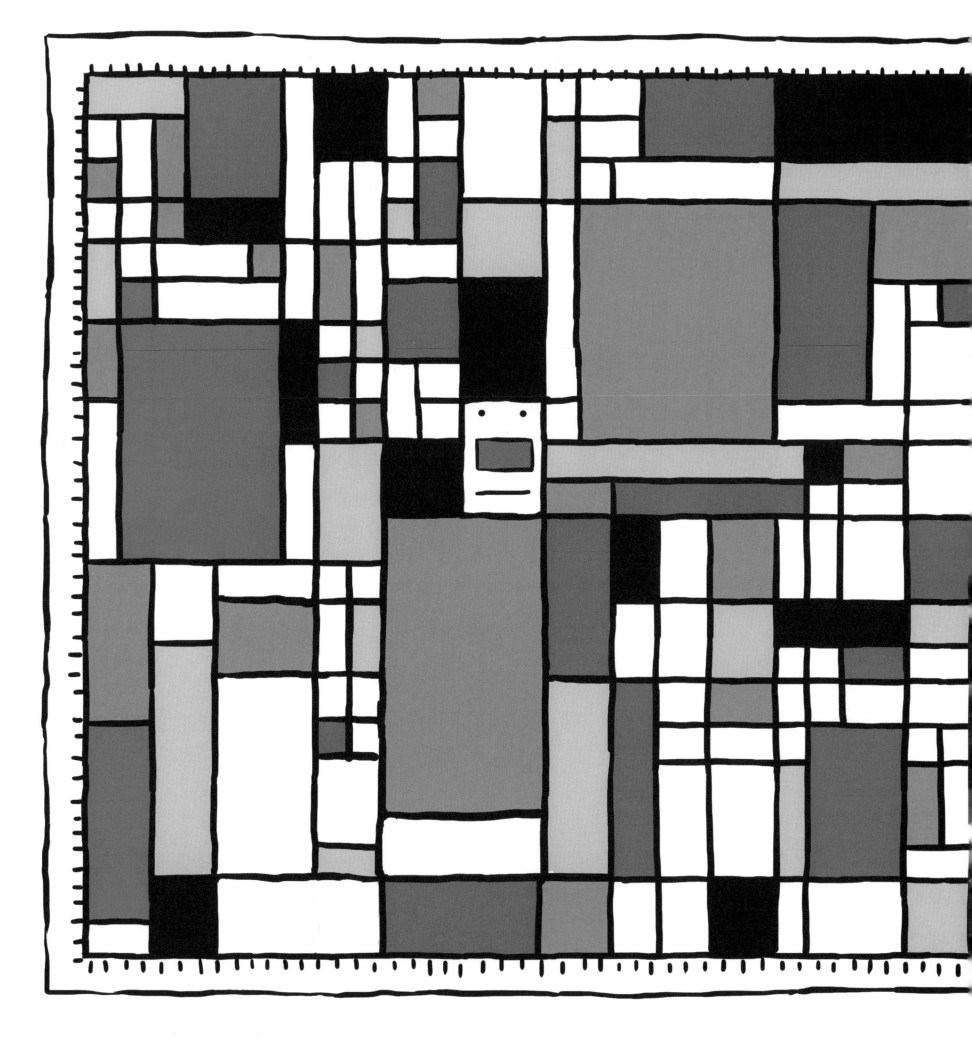

~ABSTRACT ART~

Abstract artists don't represent things we see in reality but instead create images of **their own invention** using **dots, lines, and spots**. You will not recognize any real elements in their works.

Piet MONDRIAN

created grids with black lines and then colored the inside of the squares that were formed. He used only the three primary colors (blue, red, and yellow) and the "anticolors" (white, black, and gray).

Wassily KANDINSKY

tried to represent the movement of life and the emotion of music using colors, geometric figures, lines, and spots.

Jackson POLLOCK

invented an artistic technique called *dripping*. It consists of laying a canvas on the ground and splashing it with drops and trails of paint. In those works, he was trying to communicate his feelings to us.

Sonia DELAUNAY

used circles and curved lines to create shapes of many colors that appeared to rotate.

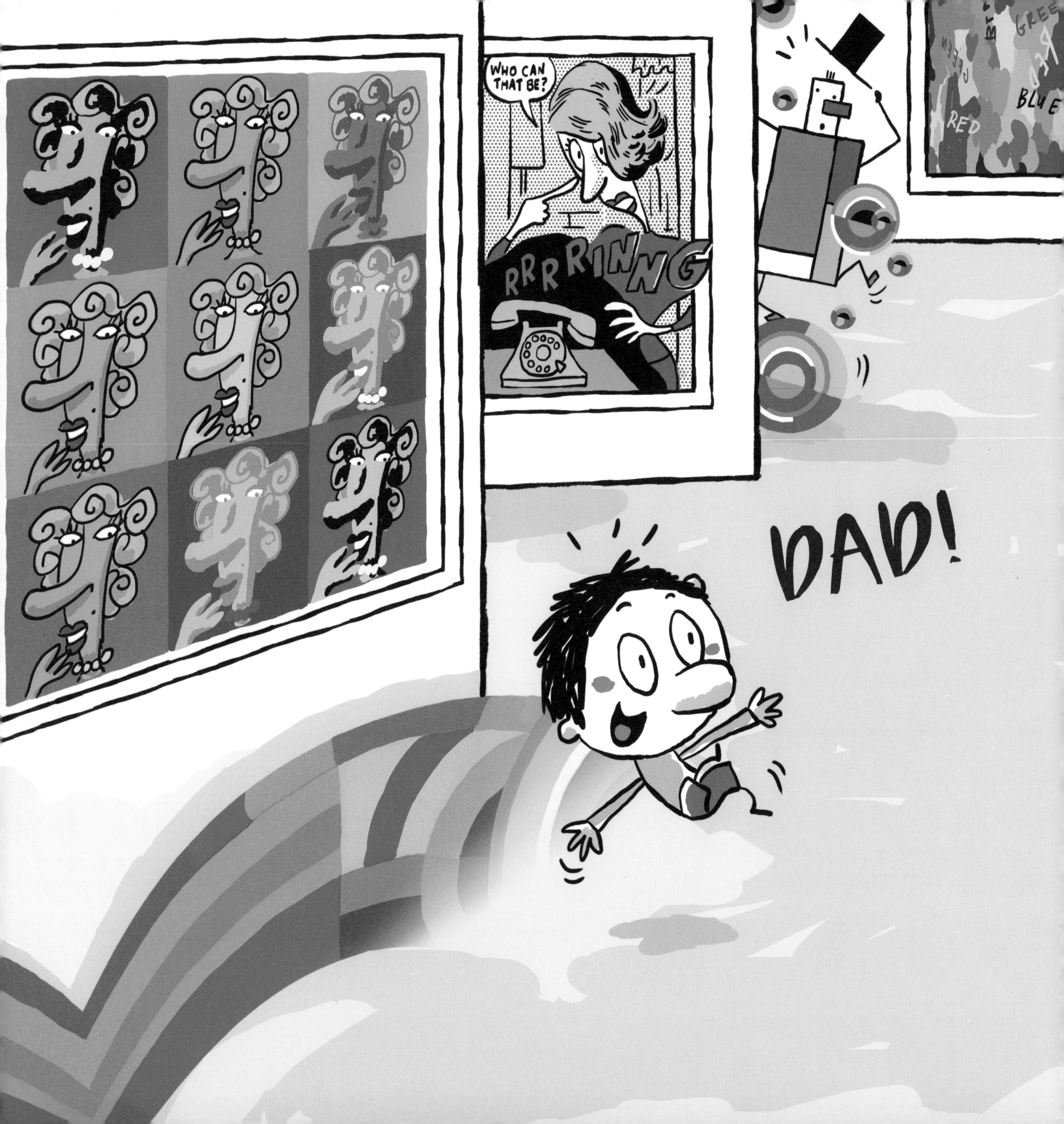

WHO CAN THAT BE?
RRRRINNG
GREEN
RED
BLUE
RED
DAD!

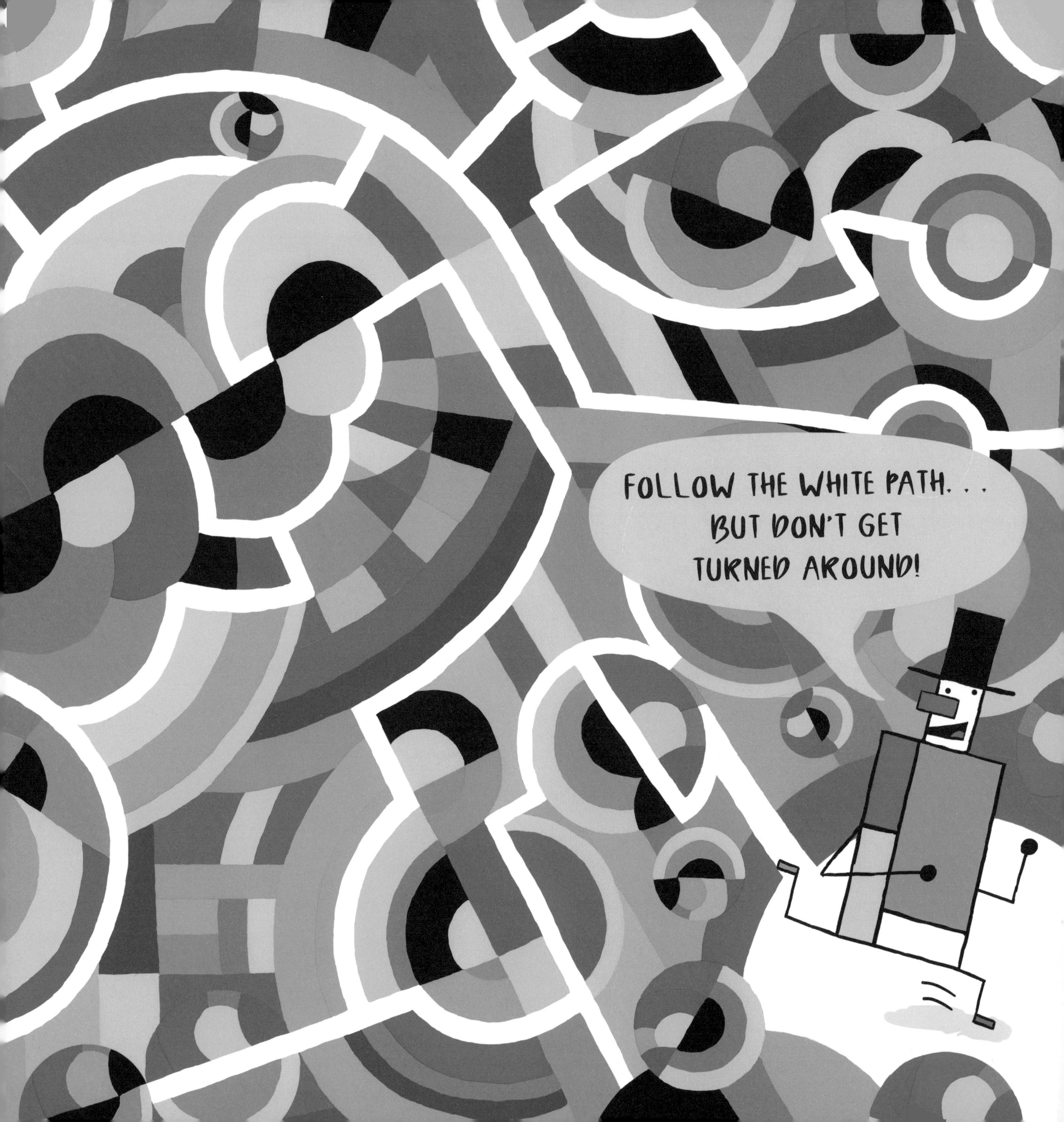
FOLLOW THE WHITE PATH. . .
BUT DON'T GET
TURNED AROUND!

~POP ART~

Pop artists recreate well-known images from **everyday life**—for example, from **comics, movies, and advertising**.

Andy WARHOL

painted portraits of famous people and repeated them several times changing the colors. He also has pictures depicting Mickey Mouse, soup cans, and soda bottles.

Roy LICHTENSTEIN

took comic strips and copied them, making them much larger. He also included the kind of onomatopoeia that is typical of comics in his paintings: Boom! Pop! Crack!

David HOCKNEY

paints scenes with people swimming or jumping in a pool, portraits of his friends, and colorful landscapes.

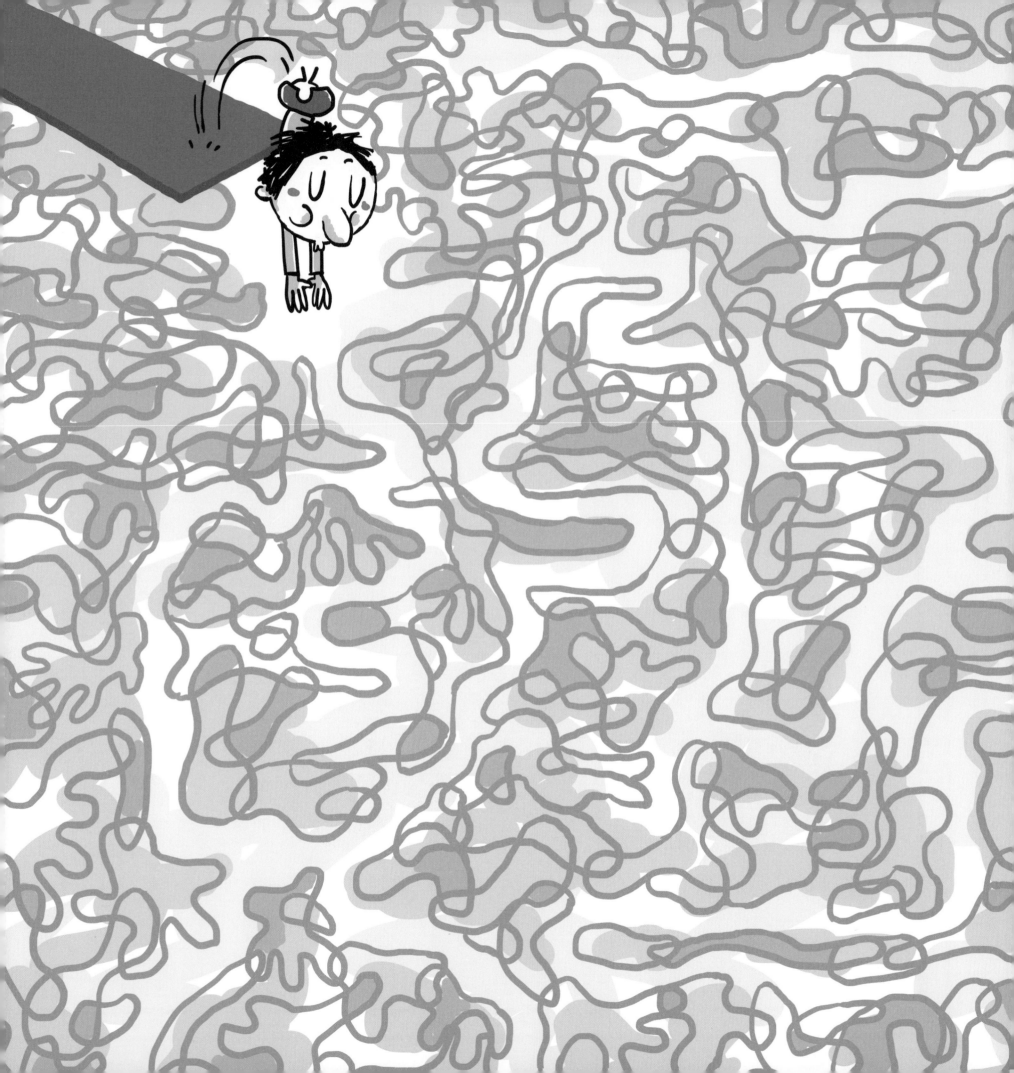